Death Becomes Us

Also by Kristen Wittman

Stone Boat

*to Vivian
you have a
wonderful daughter!*

Death Becomes Us

Kristen Wittman

[signature]

TURNSTONE PRESS

Death Becomes Us
copyright © Kristen Wittman 2021
Turnstone Press
Artspace Building
206-100 Arthur Street
Winnipeg, MB
R3B 1H3 Canada
www.TurnstonePress.com

All rights reserved. No part of this book may be reproduced or transmitted in any form or by any means—graphic, electronic or mechanical—without the prior written permission of the publisher. Any request to photocopy any part of this book shall be directed in writing to Access Copyright, Toronto.

Turnstone Press gratefully acknowledges the assistance of the Canada Council for the Arts, the Manitoba Arts Council, the Government of Canada through the Canada Book Fund, and the Province of Manitoba through the Book Publishing Tax Credit and the Book Publisher Marketing Assistance Program.

"Widow-Woman" by Dorothy Livesay is used by permission.

Cover image: *The Nose Picker* painting by Shirley Brown.

Printed and bound in Canada.

Library and Archives Canada Cataloguing in Publication

Title: Death becomes us / Kristen Wittman.
Names: Wittman, Kristen, 1972- author.
Description: Poems.
Identifiers: Canadiana (print) 20200410067 | Canadiana (ebook) 20200410075 | ISBN 9780888017314 (softcover) | ISBN 9780888017321 (EPUB) | ISBN 9780888017338 (Kindle) | ISBN 9780888017345 (PDF)
Classification: LCC PS8645.I88 D43 2021 | DDC C811/.6—dc23

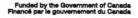

for Andrew

She should know:
Spring has surely taught her so.
She should feel
The slow, unseen
Defeat of sun
And understand
The tang in autumn air,
The fall of golden-rod.

—Dorothy Livesay, "Widow-Woman"

Contents

A Sense of Direction
Compass points / 5
Meet me at the church at midnight / 6
Break and enter / 8
Still life / 9
Sunday in July / 10
Love song of the maple tree / 12
Baseball / 14
At a garden party with Anesidora / 16
City slickers / 18
Erasing lines / 20
Last night while out jogging / 22
Upon arriving in his country / 24
Duck for cover / 25

Diagnosis
Diagnosis / 29
Construction / 30
Early morning drive / 32
Hangover / 34
Water and fall / 35
Rush hour / 36
Moonlight / 38
November without snow / 39
Let's face it / 40
Status quo / 42
Tornado queen / 43
After the fight / 46
The American dream / 48
A long drive across the prairie during harvest / 50

Love is / 52
How the winner takes nothing / 53

Death Sentence
Prognosis / 57
Apocalypse / 58
Walking to the bakery / 59
Killer whale / 60
A train passes in the night / 62
Innocence lost / 63
On the death of democracy / 64
Moguls / 66
My pledge to Ireland / 68
Grounded / 70
Run for the Roses / 71
Visiting the Guggenheim / 72
Beach holiday / 74
Till human voices wake us and we drown / 75
Visiting Berlin / 76
East, Highway 26 / 77
Confusion in the streets / 78
Lake of the Woods / 79
Hospital bed / 80
Villanelle for the ash / 81
Emergency / 82
Vigil / 84
Departures / 86
Advanced health care directive / 87

Eulogies
Space in the attic / 91
Pronouncements / 92
Afterimage / 94
Absence / 96
Dancing in the dark / 98
Isolation / 100
Siren song / 101
January 19, 2008 / 102
The wind is no longer the enemy / 104
The day they touched the sun / 106
Judicial interpretation / 108
Whistler / 113
Culture's suicide / 114
When words become power / 115
A tree falls in the woods / 116
Legal matters / 118
March 10, 2015 / 120
Black and white / 122
Final bequest / 124
Adaptations / 125
When no one else was looking / 127

From the Bones of the Dead
Pump, river / 131
Round Lake, Mud Bay / 132
Winter's funeral / 134
Journey into madness / 135

Heaven / 136
In the end our appetites will roar / 138
Pranayama / 139
Cry baby cry / 140
For the child in you / 142
Once the earth moved / 144
Moose / 146
Life as seen from an Adirondack chair / 147
The road not taken / 148
Resting in Afton, Minnesota / 149
The old, old story / 150

Acknowledgements / 151

Death Becomes Us

A Sense of Direction

Compass points

The music rattled
and shook the radio while
a crowd of people talked
I watched your eyes
like laser points
track me down
with a view
to paralyze

my mind wandered
to my afternoon bike ride
gusts of wind from the north
made mountains
of the plains

the sense of your lips
on mine a sudden diversion
of my attention
and I am surprised
by the newness of a world
that observes the gentle
caress of the wind

you whispered
north is only north
when you know
which way the river flows

Meet me at the church at midnight

       dancin' in the heat of the
       parking lot
     dancing in the soft hazy
       silvery air
we're dancing to the radio
         billie jean
   fills the air
   music filters through the
nectar of the night
rumbles over us and bursts through
    honeysuckle light

semitrailers bump and bruise
    their bulk they bounce
  a beat to match the bass
             staccato note from the grind of the
    distant train
         brushes our bodies bumps
me   into you
      sparks form in the air
        heavy with cool pockets of dew
  fireflies flicker now here now
distant   flashes of light in rhythm
      to our dancing
painting the sky
      close around us now

```
                        air vivified with the earth's sweet
       sweat a current        thick
                   we slink and slide inside
       the summer's salt and
                   laugh    wave
       to the man in the moon
                   harvest moon
                              his full flat face
                   looking down
you laugh
           looking up
                        the man in the moon sheds a lonely tear
               lands on my cheek
                   you
                        brush it away
       turn up the music
                        just so
                              we dance
```

Break and enter

The door is unlocked
so it can hardly be called a
break and enter

now you are here
   sitting on the couch
     feet on the table
       you drop crumbs

so this is it
    staring me in the face
    love a presence
in my space

you water the plants
in my absence

your farts linger
in the air
    smell of your sweat
       tickles my nose
in the bedroom

I open the windows
    in the coldest of winter

Still life

Picture near the mirror
mirror full of window
window full of snow

sitting in the grass
mirror in the picture
sun reflecting glass

couple in the picture
sitting in the sun
freckles come undone

squinting into sun
window full of snow
freckles are undone

Sunday in July

I dip my toes into pools
of sun glowing in the grass
shadow serpents
tickle my soles

I tilt my head
into your chest
drift in the space between
the beats of your heart
steady as if
time could be tamed

clouds in the sky
now form into an owl
curl about and now
perhaps mittens or
an ice cream cone
melting
into the breeze

I fall asleep
my head resting just so
your fingers tapping a drum solo
in my hair
kittens' paws whisper
in the flower beds

when I wake
heat has pressed in
the clouds have thinned
sun dapples and dances
swaddles us in
these soft grasses

Love song of the maple tree

Tap into me
all the way to the core
find the imprint of me
the stories I can't help you to see
the galaxy
written into the brains of
the birds that flutter
around me

look up into the blue
trace fingers over my branches
black spaces between melt
and freeze
prepare yourself
with gloves and galoshes
bucket and tap

let the syrup run
catch it let it pool
as inky as blood
in the bottom of the pail

you will never be ready
enough for the
splash and the speed
and the heat of me
see me through the lens
of pure maple syrup

love like mirrored glass
shines on the shadows
reveals the story
of me

turn me into maple syrup
sweet surges in the sugar of song
and count the rings of me

let me loose
put your faith in the pulse
of the flaws that flow
from the gashes of me
without pause
onto canvas
shape me soft
as syrup beads
and crystals
form on snow

Baseball

Swing and crack
ball and bat
sweaty hands
slivered and scuffed
and you are again a boy watching
us girls watching
from silver bleachers
slouched and swinging our feet
young thighs white and hard and round
inside colourful shorts
hands tucked under bums
faces like full moons
absorbing sunlight
the boys swear
back and forth
they spit
the girls dream of
the boys
dreaming of
cracking a homer past the wall
some major league city crowds yelling
the boys trip
over gangly limbs
grin get up and topple again
you the one boy always better
always quick to wink
before connecting wood to
round leather
stitches spinning
ground rule double

under the chain-link fence
once again we can spend
evenings by the dozen
summer into fall nights
giggling with all the
innocent
spitting in the dirt
and home
where heads on pillows fall
into dreams
of baseballs flying through the air

At a garden party with Anesidora

Was it passion or
tenderness when she
addressed you
backlit by a storm
brewing in the backyard
flashes of lightning
dazzled your eye
thunder clouded her question
pale Uranus crowded
in the sky

                inside and sheltered from the rain
            her words trapped
                      behind picture frames
            and the softness of lips

she wrapped herself around you
    like Cellophane

    you deflected her with poems
  but she drank you
from the outside in
      you cowered behind a philodendron

what did you think?

the storm blew itself out and
drew a line of blue across the sky
so someone opened a window
let in song
the throng of
finches and robins
in the suddenly vibrant air

City slickers

What would you say if
I said we should move to the country?
escape the city
noise and crush
pack up the china
teapot and head for the farm
lock stock and barrel

we could have five kids
and a dog
(they would all look like you)
and we'd eat wild asparagus
and strawberry juices would
stain our fingers

in the winter we'd build fires
against the cold and watch
movies on the computer
(it wouldn't be a real working farm)
in the summer we could
garden together
teach the kids all
they need to know
we'd be like
hippies only better

at dinner I'd put wild roses
on the table
(they last longer in the country)
after the kids were all to bed
we'd listen to the green rain
softly falling
and the fox bark screech
owls might frighten
the daylights out of me so
you'd take hold of my hand
and wind me up the wooden stairs
to our loft where our fingers
under printed quilts
would form teepees together
and you'd guide me through
the pretense of
living in the city

Erasing lines

Lines on the table
scratches in the old wood
a rare steak between us
vegans' scowls as distinct
as the owls hooting
disapproval
to a forgiving
prairie sky

black pools of wine
breathe in   the air
measures the distance between us
sway of curtains
drawn back
sunset stains the open panes
colours your cheeks
softens the daily glare
no longer under the stare
of city lights

the chickadee sings
its two-note query
as a challenge to
the arc of the earth

I trace with my
fingertips
along your lips
the lines around
your eyes
your brow your face
softly now
on my skin

Last night while out jogging

While out on my evening run
I contemplated you
cheating on me

not that you have I just
gave the thought some possibility
rolled it around to see
where it might lead

after all I'd like to know my reaction
would I walk away head down in distress or
chop off your genitals
or both? and what about after?
for there's always an after

we might speak at a chance encounter
at one of those dingy restaurants
with oily tablecloths
a prickly cactus
as centerpiece
now serving tapas
to emphasize portion control

you'd be with   her and
who knows for me
maybe no one maybe
I'd decide that I was happier without
the matching mountain bikes and
whole wheat bread
Saturdays shopping at the farmers' market
and sleeping in on Sundays
ball games and Frisbee
cottage on the weekend

and jogging to stay in shape
the whole time
not knowing if I'm running
from something
or straight to it

Upon arriving in his country

He offers me the chipped
enamel dipper and invites me
to drink in
his version
dripping from the cup
winding lanes lined with willows
and apple trees drooping
with desire

I lift my gaze beyond his shoulder
to the sagging roof
wood fences once rabbit-proof
and painted
solid as a grunting pig
rigid rails of rural life
now swoon and sway
for good neighbours
lost to the city

I sip again from the cup   sip
and taste cool metal
let it trickle between my lips
the psithurisms
from the trees signalling
the end of the day

Duck for cover

We walk
all the way round
Wildwood Park
we talk
words and fingers
tangle like twine

chicks taken from
their mothers
you tell me
placed in isolation
with no one to teach them
search for cover
when the shape
of a hawk
drops its shadow
overhead

I wonder

should I duck
for cover
your head a black pupil
in the sun's eye

Diagnosis

Diagnosis

Under the globe of light
your eyes shrink to black puddles
startled birds take flight

> *the way a slamming door startles the ear*
> *the sudden sinking feeling of a puncture*
> *car trouble on the coldest day of the year*

we huddle under the covers
the coldest night of the year
the river freezes over   and over

Construction

A jagged and torn concrete
road ripped apart
then covered in Tarmac
smooth as a heart

all these unruly scars
construct for me
the lines in his history
bloody scenes when someone else
helped him to his knees
left scars on everything

(the scars he leaves
will be jagged light
blinding my eyes
these scars will
stun the skies
run across the lies
hold the blight
taste like inky night
scatter heaven
my faith and trust
covered by crust
sensation deadened)

if I can believe in
what might come after
(he laughs
white lines of laughter
rough wind rubbed skin
sunlight shut in)

then I must regret
the scars I will leave
I trace with tender finger
rough raised line catching his lip
a tiny clip under the chin
these lines his epithet

Early morning drive

Streetlights flicker
tickle the tops of each passing car
the distant memory of sun
has yet to return

hum of the engine
waiting to be engaged
already in this early hour
businesses reassemble
wasps coming to life
flickering into
fluorescent buzz

traffic light turns
green to red
the rush on hold
locked in place

the panhandler
on the corner
flashes a wide grin
and flips his message board:
coins please becomes
got sum weed?

the panhandler leans against a tree
his work is done
the elm above him splays
its long and leafless branches
holding all the promises of spring
great and graceful and
easy into the sky

Hangover

The sun bleeds into morning
like a bad song
last night lurks
at the base of my skull
a damselfish
swimming through kelp

the sunrise indistinct
through murky waters

your fingers on my belly
linger
your hand tangled in seaweed
green and brown
you dive down
searching out
the soft currents swaying
gently toward my
undertow

under a sea breeze
algae blooms on the surface
green and frothy

Water and fall

He holds her in his hand
like a McIntosh apple
or more like a Honeycrisp

she looks into his eyes
a tai chi exercise

she knows if she looks deep enough
she'll plunge through
this limpid freshwater creek
all the way to the sea

where Poseidon lords over the earth
his trident thrashes the nebulous waters
inside his lonely vortex
breaking tectonic plates
the heat of the earth whirls
plumes of water into her eyes

a single leaf falls
between them
startled she withdraws
wonders how many
leaves will fall before
the trees are bare

Rush hour

On the drive to work the radio blares
soldiers returning from Iraq
in dust-covered boots
the sound of stars exploding
in their heads

(I kissed you on the forehead
before slipping into
the black morning
your hair matted from
the sweat of a night's dreams
you murmured something
I couldn't hear)

dust from the windblown deserts
chokes my vision

from the elevator to the office
muted in cool slate and tile
I pass into a world of words
alt control enter delete
computer cyclops's eye
fills with words red
struck through and
left for dead

soldiers hold cigarettes to lips
an orange glow in an empty sky
duct tape wrapped around cartridges
to keep the sand from getting in
grit under eyelids
grit lining throats
grit growing underfoot

I swipe my hand across the dust
gathering on my computer screen

desert storm snarls and sneers
and silences the howls and cries
and screech of bombs
diving from the sky

I return the headset
to its cradle
and close my eyes
where the imprint of text lingers
and angry voices ricochet
between my ears

(I stop and turn
climb back up the stairs
kiss your warm forehead
wake you gently
tell me
what was it that you said?)

Moonlight

The full moon crouches
   on the lip of the sky
   and croaks in delight

she throws her beams
      to the snowy ground

this inverted sun has
     no humility
         she knows the sinful sweetness
   of shadows
        and observes no bounds

she leaps about
      now caught in the wind
         scratching at trees scraped bare
  misunderstood

tissue clouds whisper passing by
      snatching light

while the moon scampers
         that little tease
    into the woods

November without snow

The leaves have sighed
and given over
resigned to the final fall

the trees reach their brittle fingers
to a clear sky
faint hope for today

every blade in the army of grass
shivers at each sliver
of frost

the sun's gentle touch
matters little
to their bruised and broken backs

their heads bow
in defeat
awaiting the final blow

when no one
and nothing
moves

Let's face it

Hey baby
how long you gonna nurse
this cancer thing?

working class tough
street talking temple of
wire and muscle rough
hands the man in the black leather jacket
who ate me up whole
with bear hugs
and a voice that dripped
hummingbird quips
now cowers
at the needle's approach

swapped red wine for green tea
and lentil soup
with gluten-free bread
and a handful of vitamins
and salmon oil pills
slammed back with filtered water
all part of the great
fight to stop fate

I hate lentils
let's get back to beef tenderloin
and slow-cooked ribs
evenings that linger into night
in a cool shiver
that final sliver of yellow light
holding back the night
let's forget time and what
it has in store for you

but that's easy for me to say
your health the mistress
between us now

Status quo

The bat clings to the chimney brick
his hibernation interrupted
ivy and nest ripped from the wall
seem surely apocalyptic

the sun confuses him in the sky
he is innocent of the menace he carries
he shifts his weight and waits for night
and heaves his piercing cry

he longs only to stretch his wings
to fly when the earth is warm
he must believe this too will pass
he does not want for the life of kings

a chipmunk laughs from beyond the fence
mocking his situation
never one for eternal salvation
his is fear in the present tense

Tornado queen

Clouds have formed
circles round your head

you gather them up
you swallow them whole
and claim the title
tornado queen

others watch from the outside in
amused and bemused
they see only the rip and twist
flap and clatter
as you blow by

for them
the air clears again
     for you   tornado queen
  you are caught
        in that moment
      that certain point
        moving through the
            noise of time
      when
up
  could be
    down
flat could be round
birds could be leaves
    when their feathers
    hit the ground

>   not a sound
>   makes sense
>   there's no
>   order   no
>   resistance
>
>   only the flat
>   sickening light
>   grey and obscure as cement
>
>   the music itself
>   one line
>   repeated   locked   incessant
>   no rhythm to the whirl
>   only ostinato
>   no rhyme
>
>   until one piercing
>   note
>   a clamorous call
>   a whisper in the middle of the night
>   bursts through the cloud
>   *follow the line*
>   *see the rhythm*
>   *in the rhyme*
>   the clouds part

    you see yourself as others do
    from the outside in
        the rip and twist
  of dripping heart
      the pulse and suck

hear the crow

    wrap yourself back inside your skin
    beat of the heart
      begins

blackbird flies off
into blue skies

After the fight

How cruel it is
we should have
to curl back into
the marital bed
to that place where
only moments
before the fight
our heads lay on pillows
ready to be
subsumed by
the saintly aura
of sleep

that drifting space
riding to sleep
clawed before dreams
could take hold

and now
that lying here
we should discover
a crescent moon
in the moist rush
of skin on skin
and begin again
the process of

biting into the apple
and the snake
we turn back to
the honest
lying in bed

The American dream

Never mind all that
we've got it on tape
those bastards are recorded for history
for posterity
rewind and play it again
only skip over the bit
where the poor fellow came to realize
his choice was to fight and die
or do nothing
pass over the passengers who did nothing
but cling to hope

fast-forward over the man
leaping from the burning building
his version of Icarus
hoping to sprout wings
the white shirt
flapping in the yellow sun and
disappearing into the grey smoke

turn away almost leisurely
to the good part
the bombing the tanks
the steaming piles of rubble
twisted metal
we the good   the strong
hewers of happiness
pursuers of profit

who cares who is the enemy
who the prophet
for the good fight
the wrong war   why not
pause so we can have
a happy ending

A long drive across the prairie during harvest

A curve in the road
because you always demand perfection
we fight
stones crunch against one another
sparks fly
blood in the sky

that stone
that split
second spills
onto the asphalt
bakes under the last
of the summer sun

because you are insistent
as the eternal prairie
as the grasshoppers eating the last
of the summer wheat

groundhogs that crunch
and spray guts from under our tires
with a sound
matched only by all the words
you refuse to acknowledge
in this world
that is no longer yours

so I grip the wheel
move on
follow the flow of the yellow ribbon
of the road
desire for disaster diverted

later
much later
always preferring perfection
you almost miss it
when the dip in the road hides
the harvest moon
behind cornfields

Love is

1
the owl hunting the rabbit
scream in the night
break in the habit

2
a hesitant kiss
a mutual scratching of
the acnestis

3
seeking out remedies
in sterile hallways
inchoate prognoses

4
blossoms pink confetti
carpeting green grass
whipped off the cherry tree

5
under the dappling sun
spot them and count and pick off
the cankerworms one

by one

                                                           by one
                   by one

How the winner takes nothing
(*a found poem*)

It was nothing   the beautiful
and the damned
in defence of ignorance
deference   to authority
the forgotten language

the new hero   the hostile sun
the clockmaker
the invention of the world
lovers and lesser men
to you

how the good guys finally won
allegiance in our own house
a shored up house
made in Manitoba   south of no north
I'm a stranger here
to passion   and society

the light around the body
love's body   the romantic agony
recent mistakes
the heart of a man   token and taboo
but you
only looked out the window

the self-invented man   thirty acres
the weight of the world
you only looked out the window

as for me and my house
we are exiles   the good guys finally won
and the winner takes nothing

Death Sentence

Prognosis

It was a decade marked by jet airplanes
crashing into tall buildings
silent armies slaughtering each other
with friendly fire
and devastating deaths
while commitment clawed us
with its tightening grip

still
my nose dips into
the spring air
I ride under this April sunrise
the south wind offers
a warm surprise
and slows my pace

still
everyone else sleeps
turning muzzy cheeks into
gentle pillows
while the sun dazzles
with its bursting face
dances onto panes of glass
sprinkles light onto hardwood floors
filling the house
with fire

Apocalypse

We came upon them suddenly
for though the road was surfaced
smooth and flat and grained
storm clouds lurked behind the bluff
we raced against the rain

we counted as we picked our way
among half a dozen dead
each with broken neck
white feathers coated in beaded blood
swirled about the stranded wreck

we pedalled past the birds in silence
while roar and crash and quake of
traffic never ceased
not even Yeats's giant swan
could match these metal beasts

and then the fate we feared the most
thump and roar of wind-whipped thunder
beat of wings about the head
one sucking swallow shook the night
and filled the air with dread

Walking to the bakery

We stroll along the cracking pavement
fingers linked to form a netting
splotches of orange mark the trees' disease
they stand no chance in this urban setting

the leaves not there expose the bark
branches hang in silence aching to be pruned
tired city workers start their strimmers and strum
cacophonic orchestra as instruments are tuned

buses fart along Pembina Highway
apartments frame the downtown towers
the rush and crush of shiny cars and trucks
ride the first wave of morning's tug to power

hold fast my hand and help me manage the strife
we will fumble through this as the tumours take life

Killer whale

consider
    the blue whale
as traveller

consider
    the flip of tail
        flash of blue
            sun-kissed California
            water sluicing through baleens
            Arctic circles in cold waters
            sky reflection of snow
            marble on water
        slip between icebergs
upside down
        high-rises
            huddle of fish
                dart in clusters
            clouds of surprise

consider security checkpoints
    metal detectors closed-circuit
        TV and face masks
        impertinent queries
no metal nail files now
        no corkscrews
            water bottles empty
        and pointless

      shuffle to the
next waiting point
    lugging bags of jetlag
   embracing
          with chapped lips

                and then the plane
            with a flick of the tail
         unsticks from the tarmac
       sluicing through a surface of
    cloud
     enters a sea of sky

consider
    the traveller
as blue whale

A train passes in the night

Listen to the train in the distance
there's a rhythm in the rock and the roll
the steel and sweat and memory of coal

everyone loves the far-off turmoil
the train performing its nightly tryst
the danger of speed and thrilling risk

we sleep under tired blankets
separated by that grasping gargoyle
shaping itself out of cancer's soil

up close metal grinds against metal
sparks fly with grit and grime under feet
spit and spike and furnace heat

but in the distance trains riding through
wheat fields the hope is stronger
and the days grow longer

Innocence lost

(the church spire in the distance
plagued by the plane's vibrations
pierces the cloud and tries to voice
its thoughts out loud
but we fail to hear the rhyme)

it is no longer easy
to grant the soul its symmetry
we lean our shoulders into
righteousness instead

(the setting sun a bruised apple
on the rim of the world
we are windfall passed over)

On the death of democracy

In my newly minted garden
I plant carrot seeds
found in the shed
the thin grains
grey in the new light

(I yank mint from every corner
but still it spreads
I was told to keep it
in pots
but I didn't listen)

last night's rain glistens
on the packet speared
on a stick to mark the row
on row of carrot seeds

Robertson's Orange
a real winner.

the poet tries to grow a garden
but the weeds distract
the words are backwards
reseeded and repeated
how does a garden grow?

April showers bring
May flowers

trenches and earthworms
blossoms and breezes
make snowflakes in May

what more is there to say?
we cannot reshape time
we can only rescan the rhyme

look
the barbarians stand
still at the gate

(the packet of seeds was
buried under garden gloves
and dirt-encrusted trowels
abandoned spiderwebs and dust
in the dank depths of the old shed)

do seeds expire?
can we sow them with only desire?
invasions are coming
again mark their presence with a tweet
but this time they are unseen
this time they dance among us
a simple virus
silently defeats

I should take up the call
but I cannot move my feet
I go to watch my garden grow
I watch for seedlings' sip and start
dandelion weeds
entangle my heart

Moguls

The instructor leans
           into the edge
       follow the
   line of the
fall

the woman looks out over
           crisp mountain snow
     she smells the scent
            off the tops of the pines
     snow glowing down
       in the valley below

the man points black mitt
     against blue sky
         adjusts his sleeve
    he is Adam   she is Eve

   an avalanche gun
      booms   in the distance
     glaciers sweat
          in the spring heat
     the waters
        fall

she squeezes toes in socks
           the tips of her skis
     slip past the rocks
exposed between trees

    others have come here   before
      so they search for higher points
    rust stain in the evergreen
the robin sings
      the snow glistens

she listens to the robin's playful twitter

she drops
    carves a careful turn
to this new February song
    the robin pipes its notes
an echo of
    something she has lost
      she cannot think
    she sinks

        follows the line
            of the fall

My pledge to Ireland
for James Stanley Quinn

Is it arrogant of me
to express this request?
it is my conceit

I have no intelligence
no clues to give you
my grandfather left this island
in search of wide open spaces and
and the irony of permanence
found in the shifting of
continental seasons

blonde blue-eyed sun-stained
bug-bitten consequence
of hayfields scorched by the sky
teased by possibilities
stretching to the horizon
howling skein of white winter
proves itself in snow
comes in
catalogued quantities
wind gives us our name

O Eire
slowly you spread
civilization
in your donkeys grazing
in stone-strewn meadows
aching gulls winging over
peat stacked in fields
wind bleaching beaches
licked by the wild Atlantic
waves tick the time
passed in the tickling of heather

I will stand and shout!
knock over the startled
bar stool
I will not cease
my embrace of coastal ways
nor grow weary
of proximity to the past
together let us
resist high-speed internet
and motorways!

arise and with
a hand slapped on the bar
drink the last of the whiskey
and venture out
into the cradle
of civilization

Grounded

        the view from the inn
valley heavy in mist

    the ocean
      reclaiming the land
          like lost luggage
never mind
we can't control the weather
          we sigh ourselves into rainproof gear
    point bicycles
        in the most convenient direction

      stand on pedals
    crest hill
      hold ridge a ridged
        melody from jazz
        notes on ebony
           flings down green
         and brown harmony
          into valley

lay flat the soggy map
    twist and spin until
landmarks line up
      with squiggly contours
lines within lines form
    our daily performance
inform us of the consequences
    give us a sense
      of direction

Run for the Roses

With all the bourbon baubles and bow ties
pink hats fronds and flamingos
cigar smoke swirling from
the grandstand the twisting and twirling
of conversation
shouts and jeering
tickets won
and lost and booming voices
cheering
all the loud cheering

and then the pulse and push of
noise as the sleek and sweating beasts parade
before us and the hush
and call to the post and bell and ring and rush
of muscle and whip
crashing past and clatter of the crowd
and the wave settling back against itself
waiting in sudden sullen silence
for the next race
the chase and the glory

Visiting the Guggenheim

I lean against the ledge
my back to the exhibition
moving pictures
pictures of movement
caught in stillness
painted into motion

I look down
   over the white wall
  at the people below

   I wonder why
     no artist   has thought
      to make   the perfect
       performance

        dive from the top
          with a billowing   white   shirt
      arms   spread
    to follow the spiralling ramp
  sailing past
         Crewdson and Sherman and
     Mapplethorpe
      pictures
          paintings   movie-makings

        into the grand finale

        a permanence of
brains   bones   guts
        blood and sweat

    painted onto the gallery   floor

Beach holiday

The sun burns a flashing
loonie bright in the sky

flares dance on the water
bathed in flame

bright bathing suits
flash from the blue water

purpleyellowred flowers
sing from the dark green shrubs

children leap and squeal and splash
fragrant in the sunlit water

drops arc away from their skin
glisten like shattered glass

like diamonds
their cries pierce the sun

we learn to live
in the shade

Till human voices wake us and we drown

If we tip the boat into the water and
let the first waves splash over and as one dip
our oars like spoons into cream aiming
for the mermaids and once well
into the heaving black waters rest our paddles
and rock still shall we ever move again?

the madness of motion sets in

and a woman walks
along the beach
pelicans float past white
flannel within reach
black waves cast
frothing water at the sun is it
then we are undone?

Visiting Berlin

Out on the windy cobbled street
sidewalk swept of winter's stain
wind sifting cigarette stubs
and stubborn specks of rain

the buildings seem to come unstuck
as if not rooted to the ground
shifting under billowing sky
propelled by movement all around

above the corbelled arches
towers glisten in morning light
frosted glass of sister buildings
snapping flags smart and tight

the rush of tourists tossed among
streetlights car lights give short shift
to empty observation towers
the past a swooping swift

Berlin the pace of gulped espresso
reflects the energy of renewal
sand swirls in a constant state
the only reminder of the Wall

East, Highway 26

The poets have said what there is to say
so who am I to think
I can put pen to paper and pickle
thoughts in briny ink

they've contemplated requited love
the passage of time and the seasons
they've grabbed at life and suffered death
and questioned every reason

but I could write of the passage
through copper fields cropped close
of windblown sky and sun in cloud
of winter's near encroach

a day in the fall crows on a wire
in the distance fields on fire
a fall in the day a snake on the road
blood on the shin our eyes explode

they have all said what there is to say
but they can't close the crack in the sky

Confusion in the streets

Along streets that lead
and follow as if laid down
by some wild joker intent

on avoiding the toll
we circle back upon ourselves
the church bells chime

invisible they fill the air
we change our pace
is it a race?

the cobbles reveal no line
the wet black cobbles
twist and trip

no rhythm   no rhyme
a slip   a lurch   the shining bell
when will we know

how to break the spell?

Lake of the Woods

Bird on the dock
sits peering into the lake
what's it looking for?

lightning in the distance
lights up the pre-dawn sky
lake flashes visible then gone

you are reading in front of the fire
your eyes behind reading glasses
shielded by reflected flames

gaze across the lake with me
steely glass belies what's underneath
what only the gull can see

Hospital bed

Go get a job
fill your house with art
get married
skip the middle part

swing your legs
over the edge of
the hospital bed
fluorescent lights
glisten in the sick air
          listen

the beat of that heart
always strong now falters
stand up take flight
it won't be long
soon enough
the heart won't go on

aim for the sky
above the tallest pines
leave behind the clouds
go where the sun always shines

Villanelle for the ash

What shall we do   we   the selected few?
we pulse with urges   we vacillate
all the while the sparkling beetles chew

dampened and dreary from the dew
we struggle to assimilate
what shall we do   we   the selected few?

do we simply whine and mew
about our time here? our buds pustulate
all the while the sparkling beetles chew

we've been spat out   our love outgrew
but love and time cannot articulate
what shall we do   we   the selected few?

time by hours is our purview
now so disproportionate
all the while the sparkling beetles chew

time is our enemy   we are too slow
the twitters and tweets of the birds resonate
what shall we do   we   the selected few?
all the while the sparkling beetles chew

Emergency

Drive into an unfamiliar district
in search of a main artery
where street names clot and fibrillate the tongue

it is Sunday morning
still weeks before daylight savings
when you would rather be slumbering safe under sheets
blood-filled dreams electrifying fingers and toes
instead you are awake and
the body has no choice but to close itself
over the soul

from here you cannot see your house
here the puddles pool in unfamiliar places
apartments give way to parking lots and corner grocers
trees grow larger
then smaller again without
reason yet they all have lost
their leaves to signal the season

cars drop off the Arlington Bridge
one by one
heading to the centre
roads narrowing into crash
barriers and potholes

and now traffic seems harrowing
you search your way in the bald light
the only familiar sight
the scudding clouds overhead

the hospital heaves itself into view
with its muscled buildings and self-important hue and
now there are no trees overhanging
no polite houses just wind
in the concrete whistling

and the sudden sun ferocious and frantic
it pierces the clouds
with light so remarkably bright
a surge through the soul

Vigil

I am sound asleep
I am perfectly awake

footsteps from downstairs echo
a caregiver moving about
like an intruder in our house
has somewhere else to be
a whisper up the stairway
see you tomorrow

it is the absence
it is the pain   it is the ache

you moan from deep
inside yourself
blizzard winds blow through you
I tuck the quilt up against your skin
we start again

it is the space between the words
the before   the after

I move to the chair near the door
the sunlight a warm
square on my feet
filters the dust
the words on the page trip over themselves
I close my book
and look around instead

a spider sits at the edge of the wall
under the window
she has found an ant
she is grappling
with death
I no longer wonder
how they get in here

it is the silence in the noise
the agony of laughter

you shift on the bed
it's hours until your next dose
skeleton pressed against skin
I hold my breath
until you breathe again

it is the instant when
the wind abandons the tree

I move back to my side of the bed
take some of the quilt
for me and feel the heat
coming off your body
I wonder how many more hours
before you are cold

You will hear it in the splashing of the boatman's oar
You will know when it is right to leave the shore

Departures

The tops of the trees are stained
with yellow as if
soaked in summer sun
is it coincidence that
grieving rhymes with leaving?

I fear abandonment
you know this
having stayed by my side
these twenty years
hand in hand

when we lie in bed
I stroke your hollow head
today you were not here
tomorrow you might be back
neither of us knows

it's a child's game of peekaboo
but the end of the game
is the beginning
the grieving starts
long before the leaving

Advanced health care directive

To my proxy I direct that,
in the event I experience
an irreversible, terminal condition,
make no attempts at life-saving
treatments.

fog seeps under the windowsill
insidious like perfume
the clouds plucked from the sky
tuck themselves inside the room

Keep me warm, dry, and
hydrated without intubation.
If I cannot swallow,
keep my lips moist.

we will not take a stroll today
the day's measure is not set by light
a glooming passage of time
day becomes dark before night

If it is at all possible,
I would like to remain
at home, in my own bed.
Eliminate all caloric intake.

looming in the silent air
a mourning dove's coo curled
reminds us momentarily
of the existence of the world

No more invasive surgeries.
Supply me with the
highest dosage of hydromorphone
until my heart can no longer go on;
do not resuscitate me,
for I will be already dead.

fog at midday like sleepless night
defies the most piercing look
the moment when waking
is nothing but blank
pages at the end of the book

Eulogies

Space in the attic

Are we to be the protectorate of the dead?
or must the dead make way for the living?
we who seek our daily bread

Eliot might have said
in the end it is only the beginning
that brings us round to the end

is it our calling to recall the dear
departed? as purple boots are meant to squish
mud puddles after rain in E. E. Cummings's ear

are the dead a sour lemon   our driftwood
tormenting us like an hour misplaced?
like the wise words of Kroetsch or Atwood

do the dead seek their space in an evening's sigh?
whispers with Whitman in the long tall grasses
would that the dead long to be gone and by

Pronouncements

How does one pronounce love?

you start at the beginning
with words like *like* and *attraction*
and *I'm really kinda keen*
these words are cloaks we
wrap around raw emotions
we say *I can't live without you*
but this is not a Truth
we can live without love
(though we must change the *i*)

I now pronounce you
husband and wife

perhaps actions are better evidence
for even the *I-love-yous*
get lost under the bustle of
bills and business
we held hands and worked
together on the crossword
your words in black
mine in blue
your letters opened up
new words for me
we held hands

*the doctor is here to pronounce
your husband dead*

I am polite I say *thank you*
no longer certain
to whom I speak

Afterimage

Your face a ghost
framed by the mullions
in the glass
a palimpsest on
the reflection of me
looking out from
the room to the lake
down below

I am naked
as an open window
as a meditation
I am stripped
of purpose
your death sighs
with the breath
of the budding trees
my cries rend
the sky

and when the birds
stop singing
and the clouds gather
over the surface
of the lake
the lone paddler dips
his silent oar once more
on his way to
the other side

in that stillness in
the solid granite of the
motionless water
I hear the roar the
drum your
thrum inside me

Absence

Absence is a room entered
in darkness a wine rack
emptied of bottles
a house without books

if we could see glory
in these spaces
if we could pull ourselves
through to these other
places would we
understand the universe?

the world under the ground
the ocean above the sky
the room without a sea

in the early morning darkness
after yet another restless night
spent in my cold bed
I dreamt I had
cheated on you
me a married woman
and you returned
from the dead
your absence unexplained
I choked on your presence
and woke gasping
for air

the fire stitches light
onto the walls
the coffee runs fingers
of caffeine into my heart

start   again

I turn from the fire
and face the open eye
of the window and
much to my surprise
see that the sun did rise
balancing again
in the clear blank sky

Dancing in the dark

Once they danced
    in the soft air
  moved gently
    so slowly
under Venus and the first stars
  his tan glowed in the last
    of the light
  her face pressed into
the lingering smell
        of the day
  in his soft shirt
her laugh loud and strong
     like a streak of daylight
    hovering
       in the evening sky
  his body
     a rhythm inside her

     she was learning
   even as they danced
      the lessons of abandonment
    preparing for when he would leave her
     someday

      she could picture the outline
        of his skull through thin skin
         his sharp teeth braced
           against death
            locked
          in the pit of his
          helpless eyes
      she could see this more clearly
          with every moon that shone

and then he was gone

      in the empty house
     the music bleats and blares
          at her foolish attempts
    to prepare
        chases her out
       into the night
           always that same inky sky
     hot stabs of breath

her body is out of rhythm
        lightning shatters
          the night
             leaving it darker
     than it was before

Isolation

Blue and dangling by a thread
moon hovers over passersby
lonely beacon of the evening sky
she cloaks the earth in foggy dread

where once the sun rewarded land
with vision clear and bright with mirth
suffused the air with laughing girth
stroked faces with a carefree hand

thin crowds now huddle under cold light
the moon searches with a lonesome eye
shuffles along the inky sky
resigned to move alone tonight

people denied the sun regard
blue moon in all her vanity
displaying herself in the velvet sky
wrapped up in a shawl of stars

Siren song

She is lashed
to the bow of the ship
as he foresaw
she has tied herself
and begged
the others not to listen
no matter what
she says

she sleeps on
the other side of the bed
now so as not to feel
his absence
so keenly

she has discovered
this song is for
her alone
the beeswax was
for naught
still the sirens sing

January 19, 2008
for my father

And then there was nothing
the beautiful and the damned
found again in the corner
huddled against the noiselessness
of the frozen river
locked under the pinkish hue
of the sun's relentless eye

softer your breathing now
easier maybe ready
on the bedside table leftover
poinsettias rot in their juices
while the days pass

the nurses embed your body
with drugs and you wish
out loud for one more season
in the garden
in a voice pinched by illness
beyond recognition

father forgive me for all
the years we spent waiting
for the words we thought you'd say
we weren't even a bit
prepared for this

in the darkness after midnight
your cold hand in my warm hand
as we wait for the dawn
the blazing ball of sun
coaxes only me
into day

my memory deceiving
I am still believing
that the sun
aware of your condition
hoisted itself
onto the rim of the earth
to cast its wintry eye on your
voiceless body

it was dawn and then
there was nothing
silence
the nurses came and
sent you away
the gamble was played
the final bet was made
the game was over

it was the coldest day of winter
and though there was so much more to say
there is nothing left to say

The wind is no longer the enemy
for Selma Quinn

What happened to us
where once we walked the land
with our grandfathers
whose scarred hands
pointed to the sandy hills
who drank water with milk
without coffee

grandmothers who endured the dry heat
between the wars
bent themselves like stalks of wheat
to the sun even as
the empty clouds scuffed the horizon
inured to the drought
the pain of their lost sons
the missing ones

we must become as one
with the wind
not the gentle
rustle-through-straw breeze
cat's tongue brush
against sweaty skin
fingers that tease under
shirts with caressing ease

no   we must behave
as the prairie wind behaves
when it pins you in place
rolls the stone from its space

    (the wind begins its mourning
       only when the sun has shifted
         after the day's rage has
            slipped into the leaves
           light glows under the skin
        the wind sucks itself
      thin when it senses
   the moon is a presence)

oh we will behave as the wind behaves
when it pins you in place
rolls the stone from its space

The day they touched the sun

Were they searching for
the midnight sun?
did they fly
high
enough?

not the sun
of the desert
nor of the Mediterranean
that beats back every
breath and
bleeds colour from
burnt surfaces
turns midday dark
bright light
so stark

they were longing for
the midnight sun
the sun that graces
every surface
within darkness
makes shadows
on the heart
turning skin into art

sun that yearns and licks
the surface of every living thing
and every colour
opens up
the limitless space
inside

Judicial interpretation
for Robert Kroetsch

1
A pat of butter
melting on a warm baguette
torn open steaming
then jam (strawberry)
large cup of coffee
foaming thick with cream

later a litre of *vin
ordinaire*
from an unlabelled bottle
and wedges of soft
creamy cheese
smelling of soil
and sin

allow me to accumulate
my own kind of wealth

2
The finder of a jewel may maintain trover
but the finder of a poem?
it seems easy at first to establish title
priority of time gives priority in title
but whose time?

the petrified or fossilized prehistoric chattel
found beneath the surface
half sunk amid the ooze
the facts suggest whose time
but for a poem?

for a gold ingot or
a Roman lamp of ingenious construction
or even all mines and minerals and all watercourses
the best title is ownership
but who owns the poem?

who has title to these words?
metaphysical possession
is never enough
(the bracelet was never claimed)
finders keepers the old saw goes
but what if the owner claims the article
or the noun?

this once shiny poem cast
into a public place or into the sea
abandoned or left derelict
(retaining the character of a chattel)
who is lord of this manner?
a person in possession has the right to possess
but how do you possess a poem?
who has de facto control?

the owner?
the finder?
the keeper?
it is a subject of immense disputation

3
By dint of luck
I supped with a judge
of the Supreme Court
we ate chicken à la king
she grappled over whether
a dissenting judgment
was mere literature

I bristled at *mere*
turned it into a mirror
and there
right in front of my eyes
much to my surprise
I understood
after twenty years
the *obiter dicta*
of the Puppeteers
all the questions
have already been posed
we keep drumming up
new answers

4
You said
make me into a poet
take
my telephone-pole body
and plant me in the earth
bore a hole for me
affix me on the prairie
to hold up the barbed wire
let me sing off-key
but in rhythm with the crows

I will find myself in the slop bucket
beside the pigsty
I will muck out the barns
fling the frozen dung
until my fingers become
finally numb
and sneak up into the heat
of the hayloft
to watch the kittens play

5
You planted seeds
from the catalogue
I watch them bloom and
wilt and rot
and bloom again
under the prairie sky

and in this way
I will come to understand
what the crows say

Whistler

The mountains shrouded
   in quiet fog
      settle   like a lazy dog

the memory of movement
   in the muscles of the body
tousled amid pillows

somewhere close   rain
     begins its patter

      music drifts
           through
    an open window

at the first creeping of the dark
     the village crows
   begin their bark

settle on the pines
   flapping their wings
they begin a bounce in the boughs

they dance to the music

       and the fog

           lifts

Culture's suicide

Did we notice any particular
solemnity to the day
when we supposed it was time
again to pray?
perhaps it coincided with the steady race
through vast and gilded rooms
the city below grey and covered in silt
a smell no one could place

the eleventh of September
will be something to remember
alright but only if it makes the seed
history books rendered onion skins
blistered bubbles of print
thickening inside the stock
of Twitter-feed

eventually we found the smell
the fourth estate
on fire
smoke up the stair
a final gasp of angst and despair
but it does not matter
there is no time for remorse
shirts billow in the air
follow the course
hoist yourself like a sail
be it fire or be it ice
we are now inured to
the indifference
rejoice rejoice!

When words become power
for Václav Havel

Nineteen and dumb
to the world
a new language
a rapture is born

there are garden parties
and radio-free worlds
and plastic people
moving through this universe

imprisoned and fractured
by the world the playwright
throws up the sky
hisses and spits out the sun
rends the moon
lines of distress
revolution has begun

a wall comes down
the system breaks
the poem bursts forth
seeps into
the space
flows freely over
concrete rubble

the sparrows swoop
the wind swirls
the flag flaps
the poem unfurls

A tree falls in the woods
for Liisa

The sun is on its way to sleep
earlier this evening than the last
wind howled all day
exhausting us with
its obstinacy
you locked in your bed
the prow of the boat
rocked by the wind
the breath escaping

email communication
in the middle of the night fraught
with fright
a broken neck
how can we not
stop and demand of the gods
some explanation
a simple slip in the middle of the night
is not enough

autumn calm
despite the wind
settles into cedars
who curve themselves into coolness
to mock their deciduous siblings

branch a broken neck hanging
still from the October storm
holds its dying leaves tight to itself
even as the living branches
shed themselves
to the dead
she wonders should she call someone
cut it down
before it falls

they are the dead
occupying space until the past pushes them both
into themselves and then we are complete
a broken neck here
a diagnosis there
we cannot help ourselves
but carry on

and in the silence
the elms are finally still
having shrugged off the wind's weight
leafless now they stand shoulder to shoulder
with the green and impertinent pines

Legal matters
for Armin and Stella Tefs

In her eyes the light in her eyes
a stunning silence an absence
the future a marble
is death the answer
or the question

the oak table hewn
from solid tree
its waxy covering
green with yellow flowers
now smothered in legal papers

words flow
from the lawyer's mouth
probatetitletransfer
social insurance numbers
forms to fill

the light from her eyes
grown colder than the old TV set
what does she see
now?

her lips
as they brushed his cheek
for the first time
apple blossoms exploding

she was so young and thirsty
and full of questions
how he slaked her
gave her all the answers

consider the begonias
she planted this summer
mud crusted on her hands
the moment when she rocked back
onto her heels
and wiped a smudge of mud
onto her nose and
she was nineteen
again

her last testament
statements in black-and-white
formal language
not her own
words raised from white paper
raised from the dead
so many questions

we have ceased to hold the answers
they have the answers now
they no longer need us
eyes blank
to our questions
seek and seek in search of answers
what do they see now?

March 10, 2015

A year has passed its long
and winding way
through the numbness
of summer
past the crash of fall
and the coma of winter
here I am again

now in the cruellest month

April arrives this year
in March when the cross-
country skiers
should be out with their
skeleton pals
marching through the pallor
of winter never-ending

this is the year spring
sprang from behind
sofa cushions
when no one was looking
startling me with
soft and scented air

(it would have been so much more apt
fresh blanket of snow
crushing crocuses
newly formed		plunging
mercury		zapping
trees' first sap)
but no

winter is over
life begins again
with the cruel promise
of spring

Black and white

I dream in colour
so bold
my eyes hurt
in the darkness of the morning

I tuck white long underwear
into black socks
pour white hot milk
over black coffee
cooling inside the chipped white mug

you were standing behind me
in last night's dream
wearing your bright red
checkered shirt and a light blue scarf
wrapped inexplicably round your neck
whistling and laughing
at something I could not see
you were so happy
so carefree

black crow prances about
a fresh thin blanket of white snow
searching for berries
or the guts of squirrels

the November sun seeps from the sky
reflecting a river of melted
mercury that slips
past me on its way
downtown and then on
to disgorge itself into Lake Winnipeg
and on again
north to the shores of the Hudson Bay

I read stories of the dam
under construction
Keeyask the black and white birds
that swoop over the rippling river
under the sun's watchful eye
black birds swoop
in the white sky
forth and back
white and black

Final bequest

To my niece
the old piano
in the dining room
dust it off
and make it sing

to my nephews
my collection of bird
paintings
photographs
and severed heads

and to you
this bottle of wine
dust it off
release the cork
and pour the length
of it into these
crystal glasses

swirl until purple
bursts on the brim
touch the goblet to your lips
on this cool morning
and listen

        for the robin's whistle

Adaptations

You once told me
that if we are made to listen
we may hear life's deep irony
a crease in the crust of the earth

I balance on my skis at
the top of the hill
and wait for my hammering heart
to smooth itself into
a drum beat

above me a hawk plays
in the shadow of a plane
improbably moving through the sky
on its way to touch down

unlike most others I know
I am a lover of winter
I crave the snow
and become irritable when
the skies remain flakeless
in November

the firs surround me with
their pine scent
I am soothed by the steady silent
sweep of snow
falling around me

it is five years since you died
six since the March I started skiing
to pass the days watching you
recover from a surprise heart attack
I suppose all heart attacks come as a surprise
but when dying of cancer
you don't expect you might die
from something else

at night I dream of
flying across icing-sugar snow
at impossible speeds
I ski early in the morning darkness
deprived of sight
I mimic that feeling of flight
we are the most adaptable species
it is said

later I will make my way to Starbucks
and finally take the time
to update your account
put it in my name so the baristas
stop calling me Wayne

and another piece of you
will be gone for good

When no one else was looking

It happens upon
retreat from the dinner table
to a more comfortable chair
within view still
of smudged wine glasses
stained purple
the candles toppled soldiers
among the heel of bread
and clatter of china plates

when the music
lingers in the head
the birds' twitter
signals evening's end
and the song   begins
shaping itself into night
one comes then
to a sense of ending

From the Bones of the Dead

Pump, river

When in the darkest depths of night
where death no longer squats in shadows
but steps out boldly to the light

the water's dried and done its course
consumed inside its bed
and the river at last is drained of force

after all the years of all the knowing
that this moment should come to pass
and push me into grieving at the going

in readiness I block off the hour
float my raft of wishes round the room
alone in this my outcast tower

where I always prepared to cower
(so long a life awaiting death)
behind the pillars of pride and power

time that great betrayer of us all
has started the liquid flowing
even as I prepare myself in mid-fall

what is this sudden rush of new emotion?
a prime to start the pumps again?
with greed I drink this puzzling potion

and sudden oh so suddenly I'm free
a life of death no more a life for me

Round Lake, Mud Bay

After the funeral
I made promises to myself
and time for once stood still

the comforting cloak of
grief granted me
a certain sense of peace

but then the curl of lock
a silver sliver
breaks my meditation

in the blue sky
my will dissolves
the sea in the eyes

we examine the painting
together and to my surprise
yellow sky could be sunset or sunrise

and in the formation
of geese moving south
or maybe moving north

these shoulder seasons
so similar to each other
spring and fall

it is in this moment
the beginning and
the ending is all

Winter's funeral

Rot and decrepitude
mark spring's limp onto the prairie
the equinox long since passed

the first signs the fiery ferocity of sun
dog turds exposed in snow
like tumours on a patient's skin

two old snowmen clutch at each other and brace
against the steady blow from the south
and a head splotches on its face

the children are indifferent
focused on ever more urgent wars
they fail to notice the decapitation

a skinny skeleton skis past
struggling with the last of the sticky snow
a sombre solemn service

winter's funeral concludes with a robin's note
and the cinnamon scent of sap
sweeter than song thrums through the trees

Journey into madness

When the first frost bites into the last of summer's begonias
and the moon wanes and the tears crease
let the memories be released

when the leaves quit the trees and snow speckles the sky
do not question every visit
allow me to absorb the spirit

when you reach deep into me with hands warm and strong
splay your fingers round my heart
hold tightly for the healing start

Heaven

Why is it
when we reach the edges
of the spectrum
it is the sky
we seek

sky over ocean
sunset-streaked
gaping blue or
peeking from the
cover of
quilted cloud

filled with
red-winged blackbirds
and blue jays
filling us with
the proposition
that there is
some greater being up there
making it all
work out
preposterous but
persistent

so we turn to it
fill it with gods
and heaven

pull it in and
plant it   smack   in your eyes

In the end our appetites will roar

Spring and nature
clears its throat
tugs at leaves with a hoary smile
randy as a stoat

winter's anxieties
dissolve into muddy puddles
squirrels leap from bough to nest
in search of furry cuddles

can it be I'm awake again
to nature's clamorous throng?
the slap and tickle of melting snow
the whip of the cardinal's song

Pranayama

When I watch blue flame
dance across the candle
I dream of waves
licking the sand
and tickling my toes
in retreat
I dream of breathing underwater
of breath as deep as
flame's beginning
perhaps there is a symmetry
between ocean and fire
a partnership   a noose
a strangle of desire
between the flicker
the flip and the lip
we learn to breathe again

Cry baby cry

Do you know
last week I had a dream
a simple dream
where a song played in my head
a song with the lyrics
cry baby cry

when I woke up the song was
still in my head
but I couldn't place it
all day the words ran circles round my head
to a certain tune that I knew was
not recent not a song
I'd heard for the first time
in the last few days but also
not a song that I'd known since I was a child
it was somewhere in between
a song that was maybe by a band
that Andy introduced me to
my son who was leaving tomorrow
for a new job and another life

the son I said *I love you* to
when I dropped him off after supper
our last supper it was lamb
sirloin do you know you can sear a lamb sirloin
and roast it on the barbeque it is a fine
and excellent cut of meat

and I served homemade mint sauce as an accompaniment
and he ate a lot and said how good it was
and I drove him back to his apartment
where he'd lived these last few years
after his father died
and said *goodnight* and *drive safe to Calgary*
and I said to myself it's only Calgary
he's one flight away
and there were no tears

but on Saturday
when I woke up this song was
running through my head again
and I couldn't quite place the artist
or the lyrics
but it didn't matter

I stood at the window
and cried

For the child in you

A sudden suppressing
sense of circles
surrounds me
falling back inside myself
into the pain of the moment
like the discovery of a lie
that I had always believed
a broken tree
lying across the path
its insides rotted out
only the hollow bark to hold it up
against the wind

you yank me back
back to where
I am alone and naked
inside time
back to where a single doubt
calls my entire existence
into question

take my heart
open it up
thread by thread
inside there is
a little rubber bouncy ball
like the one you had as a child

throw it
against the pavement
watch it bounce
high into the sky
into the pattern of clouds
pick a cloud
bring it down
and sew my heart back up again

Once the earth moved

With the stubbornness of stones
      we resist the message in our bones
refusing any new perspective
      we wrap ourselves in our own invective
yet we know the story of the stone
      that moved we're told from love alone

not so much a stone as a boulder
      moved by God's imperious shoulder
only after death the story tells us
      when all was grief and anger from the masses
can the message still deliver
      in this world about to smoulder?

weary of these thoughts I headed for the desert trail
      whereupon a placard on a rail
told me of the mountain story
      its formation and its glory
boulders sliding as if ships at sail
      now spiked by saguaro our new holy grail

I stood amazed at the adaptations
      bubbling in this desert station
plants that wait five years for rain
      before they drop their seeds to sow again
islands of Darwinian isolation
      refusing to succumb to indignation

if we could see the danger of relief
 founded on some false belief
perched on the slope of this green hill
 what emotion sponsors the renewal?
with the loss of every leaf
 we must prepare ourselves for grief

today it's Australia burning that behooves
 us to gamble on a countermove
if we set ourselves a pace
 within this scarred and lonely space
will life teem on every knoll?
 will we help the stone to roll?

Moose

Moose crashes through bushes of berries with poise
mouth full of reeds stripped from the marsh
moose is not disturbed by the noise

moose has no need for the owl's advice
she knows the waltz of the waters like a Russian empress
she understands the thickness of ice

nor is she bothered by anxiety
overpopulation is not her concern
her legs give stature to the snow-covered lea

she winks at the stars and is not amazed
when they peek from behind purple mountains
freed of the shyness of dusk to return her gaze

nor will she consider the symbolic stages
in the flickering arc of a dying star
in the deepening night the decay of ages

Life as seen from an Adirondack chair

We listen to the cicadas'
high-wire rhythm
black-eyed Susans peek
through the knot in the fence
we are inert under
the thick slick air

we switch chairs
for a difference in perspective
amused by the cardinal's song
time's tireless march evident only
in clouds stained by the setting sun
a smear of raspberry jam
on the white breadth of the sky

we contemplate the size
of robins in the fading light
they grow fat on the worms
in the garden the chipmunks
grow fat on the strawberries
we settle deeper into our chairs
knowing the jet stream
will dim soon enough

even as the monarch
lets its wings unfurl
we resist the passage of time
and I remain astonished
by the beauty of the world

The road not taken

It's time to stroll through
a room in the house you never built
peer through imaginary windows

look out over the lake
in which you never swam
but talked as if you might

sit at the wrought-iron table
that might have balanced on a cobbled street
in front of a Parisian café

turn to the arguments that never drifted
up from the troubled mist
of the river that was never there

ask yourself how it is
you are here
        somewhere not there
it is all
in all events
        everywhere

Resting in Afton, Minnesota

In this early August hour
corn and flax   sunflower and wheat
feel the pulse of summer's power

through open windows children's squeals
drift over tangled bodies' heat
porches creak under church bells' peals

dragonflies and cicadas conspire
successfully with the siren beat
and drench themselves in earth's desire

The old, old story

As the finch needs the thistle
the ear the robin's whistle
as the squirrel needs her tail
so the train the iron rail

the chipmunk and the nut
the workload and the rut
courage founded in despair
jasmine in the evening air

a freeway for every sin
a sleepless night for every gin
love shines through the rust
indelible as lust

caffeine in every vein
when life begins again
no matter we resist
the sunset in every kiss

the swamping of memory
the saltiness of the sea
the sunlight in the dust
death becomes us

Acknowledgements

When writing acknowledgements, does one thank the inspirations for the poems? Those who shaped the poems in this book, who have gone through a similar experience of losing a loved one, or the loved ones I've lost? If so, I thank Liisa and Jodi, Grandma and Grandpa, Stella, Alison, my mother, my father and, of course, Wayne, my muse, my love, my teacher, my lost soul. I would be remiss, however, if I did not extend a plethora of gratitude to Dennis Cooley, the first and most patient of readers, to Di Brandt, my whip-cracking editor who refused to be bruised by my puns, to Andrew, who has given me more support than he could ever understand, and to Dave, the surprise in my eyes and, it turns out, one helluva good reader. A poet has no purpose without an audience and no story without experience. Thank you for being there for me.